350 Fabulous Writing Prompts

Thought-Provoking Springboards for Creative, Expository, and Journal Writing

by Jacqueline Sweeney

SCHOLASTIC

PROFESSIONAL BOOKS

New York • Toronto • London • Sydney • Auckland

Acknowledgments

I'd like to thank Carol and Paul Cooper for their generous computer gift, which has and will continue to save me many, much-needed hours for my writing.

Thanks also to my editor, Liza Charlesworth, for her skill and advice concerning the preparation of this manuscript.

And as always, thank-you to my agent, Marian Reiner, for her good-hearted support and expertise.

Cover design by Vincent Ceci
Cover illustration by Stephanie Peterson
Interior design by Frank Maiocco
Interior illustrations by Kate Flanagan

ISBN 0-590-59933-X

Dedication

This book is for my parents, Norma and John Sweeney,
for all the questions they couldn't answer; and for those they did.

Table of Contents

How to Use This Book

Who is the fairest person you know? Is it always bad to lie? What is the toughest decision you ever had to make? What made it so difficult? A friend asks you to keep a secret about his or her plans to do something dangerous. Is it okay to tell the secret to an adult? If you could change one thing about your life to make it better, what would it be? If you could make the sky rain anything at all, what would it rain? These are just a few of the hundreds of thought-provoking questions you'll find in this book.

The questions are designed to honor students' imaginations, sharpen their critical thinking skills, and encourage them to make sound decisions. And while I organized the questions into chapters that have natural curriculum ties, I encourage you to "jump the fence" and share questions with students in surprising ways. For example, during a literature discussion, dip into the Did You Ever? chapter and ask kids to ponder Abraham Lincoln's reflection on enemies—hey, why wait for history class? Or give students an early morning thinking-skills workout by writing on the board a question from the Tough Decisions chapter. Tell your students they have five minutes to ponder the dilemma, and then launch a rousing class discussion even before the clock strikes nine. Here are some more ways to use the questions in this book:

• Prepare sheets of ten questions for students to use as journal prompts. Students can tape your list to the inside of their journal covers. Give them new sets of questions each month.

• Set up a Creative Thinking learning center in your room. Provide students with a stack of index cards, on each of which is a question for them to talk about. Schedule groups of students to discuss a question as a group, or schedule pairs, or invite students to visit the center solo, and write their responses in a journal.

• Tailor a learning center to a specific subject, and link questions from this book to a hands-on activity. A science station about oceans, for example, could really make waves if it's enhanced with questions from the Animals and the Environment chapter.

• Use the questions as tools for assessment, in any subject area.

• Devote an hour or two each Friday to celebrate kids' intellects and their imaginations. Give children free rein to choose a question and the mode of responding to it. From silly soliloquies about how to improve one's baby brother, to impassioned group debates on white lies to, one-act plays about our government, these Friday sessions will hone children's thinking skills dramatically.

• For an individual project, ask students to answer a question non-verbally—through music, dance, or art.

• Have students grapple with questions in the School Situations chapter to help you define a respectful classroom community.

• Invite students to select a question from the Feelings or Early Experiences chapters, and then schedule a time to share their thoughts with you one-on-one. These conferences let children know you really value their experiences and their concerns.

Additionally, as you use this book, please keep these ideas in mind:

• Model good listening habits for students. Be aware of how attentively you listen to children, and try to develop ways to spend more time listening to them.

• In-class discussions, students' writing, and informal chats let children know their opinions count—but their opinions must be based on reasons.

• Notice how you respond to children's ideas during discussions. Do your responses encourage creative thinking and inspire open discussions? Are there ways you shy away from students who "think outside the box?" Jot down a few open-ended responses to try out.

• The more you show children that there is often more than one correct answer to a problem, the more confident they will be in their ability to think independently.

Remember, the two most important things we can do as teachers are to help children think for themselves and to instill in them the belief that their thoughts and feelings matter to others. I hope this book will help you accomplish both of these critical goals.

If You Could Change...

⌐1⌐

If you could change one thing about your life to make it better, what would it be?

⌐2⌐

If you could change one thing in the life of one of your relatives to make it better, who would you choose and what change would you make?

⌐3⌐

If you could change anything about a brother or sister of yours, what would it be? Do you think your brother or sister would want to change anything about you?

⌐4⌐

If you could change one thing about the weather in your part of the country, what would it be?

⌐5⌐

If you could make it rain anything except water, what would it rain? (For example, rootbeer, gumdrops, goldfish, etc.) How would this rain affect people and the environment. Be silly if you wish!

⌐6⌐

If you could make it snow anything but snow, what would your snow be made of? How would it affect people differently than real snow? Would children or adults enjoy this snow the most?

⌐7⌐

When candidates are campaigning for office, each party (Republican or Democratic) spends a lot of time and money trying to make its opponent look bad on television, radio, and in magazines and newspapers. Can you think of a better way for candidates to campaign? If you could make three rules for candidates to follow during their campaigns, what would these rules be?

⌐8⌐

If you could be any TV mother or father when you grow up, which one would you be? What qualities made you choose him or her?

～9～

If you could be any TV character at all, who would you be? Why?

～10～

If you suddenly became a TV executive, name two television programs you would cancel. Explain your reasons for canceling these shows.

～11～

If you could create two new shows for television, what kind of shows would they be (sports, situation comedy, exploring nature, etc.)? Describe the shows and explain your reasons for adding them to the schedule.

～13～

If you could join any family on television, which family would you join? Who is your favorite person in this family?

～14～

If you had the power to turn yourself into an animal anytime you wish, which animal would you choose to turn into?

～15～

If you could change one thing about the United States, what would you change (for example, a law, the people, or the environment)? Explain your answer.

～16～

Some people are happy with their appearance. Some are not. If you could change one thing about your appearance, what would it be? How do you think this change would affect your life?

～17～

If you could suddenly give yourself a talent that you don't presently have, what would it be?

～18～

If you could change places with anyone in your family, who would you choose to be? What's the first thing you would do as that person?

Tough Decisions

❧19❧

In 1995, New York State reinstated the death penalty for the first time in 18 years. Do you think the death penalty is a good thing for a state to have? Explain why you do or do not feel this way.

❧20❧

Have you ever been told you can't do something because you are a girl or a boy?

❧21❧

Were you ever asked to keep a secret you didn't want to keep? How did it make you feel?

❧22❧

Sometimes secrets are okay to keep, such as not telling your sister about a surprise party planned for her. Can you think of any secrets that aren't okay?

❧23❧

Is a lie always bad? Can you give an example of a lie that isn't bad?

❧24❧

If you had to choose between being ugly and rich or beautiful and poor, which would you choose? Give the reasons for your choice.

❧25❧

Do you think boys or girls should not learn to do some things simply because of their gender? For example, some people think girls shouldn't play football or boys shouldn't be stewards on airplanes.

❧26❧

What's the toughest decision you ever had to make? What made this decision so difficult?

❧27❧

Do you believe states that have the death penalty make criminals think twice before committing crimes?

⌒28⌒
Name two recording artists whose music you really like. What are your reasons for liking this music?

⌒29⌒
A woman driving through McDonald's spilled hot coffee on her lap and sued for a huge sum of money. The judge awarded her $640,000. Some people question whose responsibility spilled coffee should be: McDonald's, for making it so hot or the woman's, for not being careful. What do you think?

⌒30⌒
The O.J. Simpson trial lasted a long time. Do you think it would have taken so long if Mr. Simpson wasn't famous?

⌒31⌒
Do you think court hearings should be broadcast on television? Why or why not?

⌒32⌒
Which do you think is more important, how a person looks or the way he or she acts towards others?

⌒33⌒
Have you ever become friends with someone who didn't treat you nicely? Why did you do this? (Was this person more popular than you, better looking, etc.?)

⌒34⌒
A proverb from Uganda states: "Words are easy, friendship hard." What do you think this proverb means?

⌒35⌒
What's the most interesting gift you've ever received?

⌒36⌒
If someone offered you a million dollars to swim in a tank for five minutes with a great white shark, would you do it? Why or why not?

⌒37⌒
If you discovered that your little brother or sister was stealing money from your mother's purse, what would you say to him or her?

☙38☙

If you are with someone who is caught stealing, even if you are innocent, you could be prosecuted too. Knowing this, if you were in a department store and you saw your best friend steal a piece of jewelry, what would you do?

☙39☙

Your little sister is overweight. Everyday on the way to school a group of children tease her and call her "fatty." What might you do to make these children realize they should stop teasing her? What could you say to your sister to make her feel better?

☙40☙

Sometimes we jokingly call people names that really hurt their feelings. Have you ever been innocently called a name that hurt your feelings? Have you ever heard someone else called a name that could have hurt his or her feelings, even if the person didn't show it?

☙41☙

Did you ever hear someone call one of your friends a hurtful name about his or her appearance? What would you say to this person if you could speak your feelings right now?

☙42☙

If you were asked to advise people *not* to smoke, what reasons would you offer to convince them?

☙43☙

If your friend thinks she sings like Mariah Carey but she really sounds like a squawking goose, would you tell her? What would you say if this same friend wanted to join your singing group?

☙44☙

One of your teachers just returned from lunch and doesn't know he has a piece of lettuce on his front tooth. Some students are beginning to laugh at him. Would you tell him about the lettuce? Why or why not?

☙45☙

Someone in your class copies other people's work and passes it off every day as his or her own. He or she is making better grades than you are, even though you work very hard and do all your homework yourself. Should you tell? If not, what can you do to make yourself feel better about this situation?

Animals and the Environment

⌒ 46 ⌒

If you saw a kitten by the roadside, what would you do? If you knew your parents wouldn't allow you to keep the kitten, what other actions might you take to help it?

⌒ 47 ⌒

Pretend you are a contractor who has just been offered a huge sum of money to build an amusement park. Before you start bulldozing trees you discover that the site chosen for the park is a habitat for a rare species of owls. If you are the only one who knows about the owls, what would you do?

⌒ 48 ⌒

Do you think it's okay for scientists to experiment on helpless animals, even if the experiments might eventually save human lives?

⌒ 49 ⌒

How many endangered species of animals do you know about? Do you think there's anything someone your age can do to help these animals?

⌒ 50 ⌒

Do you have a favorite endangered species that you'd like to protect? What do you especially like about this animal?

⌒ 51 ⌒

Endangered species cannot speak for themselves. Often they are confused about the changes in their environment which threaten them. If you could be the voice for an animal whose life or habitat is in danger, what animal would you choose to speak for, and what would you say to the world? (Speak in the first person, I, as if you are the animal, and tell what animal you are, where you live, your problem, your fears, what you wish to have changed, and so on.)

⌒ 52 ⌒

If you could be the voice of any part of the environment (the ocean, ozone layer, etc.) what would you say to people? (Describe the most beautiful or important part of yourself, and be sure to include what you fear from mankind.)

⌒ 53 ⌒

Social scientist Havelock Ellis said: "The sun, the moon, and the stars would have disappeared long ago, had they happened to be within reach of predatory human hands." Do you agree with this statement? Give your reasons for agreeing or disagreeing.

⌒54⌒

Can you name three dangers to the environment that some people use every day in their homes without realizing the danger?

⌒55⌒

What can someone your age do to help increase people's awareness about recycling at home?

⌒56⌒

British conservationist Gerald Durrell said: "Anyone who has gotten any pleasure at all from nature should try to put something back." What is your interpretation of Mr. Durrell's idea?

⌒57⌒

Can you name two things in nature that give you and your family pleasure? How might you give something back to nature for the pleasure it has given you?

⌒58⌒

Does your school recognize and celebrate Earth Day? If so, what does it do?

⌒59⌒

Do you have any ideas about how Earth Day might be celebrated in the future (for example, planting a new tree or cleaning up the area around your home or school)?

⌒60⌒

Can you name two products dangerous to the environment that might be found in someone's garage?

⌒61⌒

Can you think of any ways that you or your family may be harming the environment? List them, then tell how you might improve the situation.

⌒62⌒

Do you think our environment would be in such danger today if more people had started thinking about conservation and recycling 50 years ago?

⌒63⌒

"We are tomorrow's past," says Mary Webb. What do you think she means in terms of how we treat animals and the environment right now?

⌒64⌒

How do you think the recycling and conservation methods you adopt today will make the world better for your children?

⌒65⌒

If you could make up your own saying or slogan to express how you feel about saving the earth and its resources, what would it be?

Did You Ever?

⌐66⌐
Did you ever say something you regret to someone in your family? How would you change the words if you could resay them today?

⌐67⌐
Have you ever done a kind act that no one knew about? How did it make you feel?

⌐68⌐
Did you ever apologize for something you didn't do? Explain why.

⌐69⌐
Did you ever get blamed for something you didn't do? How did it make you feel?

⌐70⌐
Did you ever willingly take the blame for someone else's actions? Do you regret doing it?

⌐71⌐
If you are a girl, did you ever learn to do what some consider a "boy" activity, like climb a tree or play football, better than the boys?

⌐72⌐
If you are a boy, did you ever learn to do what some consider a "girl" activity, like cook or baby-sit, better than the girls?

⌐73⌐
Abraham Lincoln said: "Am I not destroying my enemies when I make friends of them?" Did you ever have an enemy who later became your friend? How did this happen?

⌐74⌐
Did you ever stop speaking to someone? Why? How long did your silence last? If you could handle this situation differently, how would you handle it?

⌐75⌐
Groucho Marx once said: "I find television very educational. Every time someone switches it on, I go into another room and read a book." Which do you prefer, reading a book or watching television?

～76～

Did you ever have a nasty rumor started about you that wasn't true?

～77～

Did you ever turn off the television so you could read instead? Name and describe the book.

～78～

Did you ever have a day when everything went wrong? Describe this day from start to finish.

～79～

Did you ever get the giggles when you didn't want them? Describe what happened.

～80～

Did you ever make a gift for someone instead of buying one? If so, what did you make? How did it make you feel to give this gift?

～81～

Did anyone ever make a present for you instead of buying one? What was it? Did receiving this home-made gift make you feel differently than if the gift had been purchased from a store?

～82～

Have you ever won anything in a contest or drawing? What was it? Were you surprised that you won?

～83～

Did anyone you know ever do anything dangerous? What was it? Did they do it on purpose or by accident?

～84～

Have you ever done anything dangerous? What was it? Would you do it again?

～85～

Did anyone ever save your life? Tell about it.

～86～

Did you ever have a good friend who later became your enemy?

The Future

⊛ 87 ⊛

If you could close your eyes and see yourself ten years from now, what do you think you'd see? What are you doing? Do you have a job? If so, what is it?

⊛ 88 ⊛

If you could magically turn yourself into any age in the future, what age would you choose to be? Why would you like to be this particular age? Describe what you think you would look like.

⊛ 89 ⊛

Cancer research scientist Charles F. Kettering said: "My interest is in the future because I am going to spend the rest of my life there." How does this quote apply to people your age?

⊛ 90 ⊛

Have you ever thought about what classes you'd like to take when you're in high school? Have you ever thought about what activities you'd like to participate in (sports, newspaper, chorus, etc.)?

⊛ 91 ⊛

Do you think you'd like to get married some day? Why or why not?

⊛ 92 ⊛

If you plan on getting married in the future, do you think you'd like to have children?

⊛ 93 ⊛

What kind of parent do you think you'd be (strict, permissive)?

⊛ 94 ⊛

Jacqueline Kennedy Onassis once said: "If you bungle raising your children, I don't think whatever else you do well matters very much." Do you agree with Jackie Onassis? Why or why not?

⊛ 95 ⊛

Some people decide they never want to have children. What do you think of this choice?

❧96❧

What else besides money is important to consider when choosing a career?

❧97❧

Have you ever told anyone what you'd most like to do when you grow up? Have you ever thought about it?

❧98❧

Have you ever thought about what you'd most like to do when you finish high school? Is there anything you can do right now to prepare for your future plans?

❧99❧

Abraham Lincoln said: "The best thing about the future is that it comes one day at a time." Do you think this is a comforting statement?

❧100❧

If you suddenly woke up after a ten-year sleep, what would be your first request? Then what would you do?

❧101❧

What do you think your neighborhood (or town) will look like in 20 years? Will it be changed? If you live on a farm, do you think it will stay the same?

❧102❧

Supreme Court Justice William O. Douglas once said: "I hope to be remembered as someone who made the earth a little more beautiful." Think carefully, then complete three sentences of your own that begin with the phrase: "I hope to be remembered as someone who..."

❧103❧

Can you name three famous people who have inspired future generations by their achievements? It could be a historical figure, a scientist, a sports figure, etc.

❧104❧

Can you think of someone who isn't famous who has inspired you? Explain how this person has inspired you?

❧105❧

Do you think cars will be used 100 years from now? If so, what features will they have? If not, describe your "vehicle of the future."

School Situations

❧106❧

If your principal told you you'd been chosen to create two new after-school activities for your classmates, what would these activities be? (Your choices might include a sport, a hobby, an exploration of a special or unusual subject area, etc.)

❧107❧

The television character Barney, the purple dinosaur, was created by an elementary school teacher to make learning more fun and interesting for her students. Describe an imaginary character you might create to make learning more fun for your class (include a description of size, clothing and whether your character is an animal, an object, or a made-up person).

❧108❧

If you were the principal of your school, what's the first new rule you would make?

❧109❧

In China, children go to school on Saturdays. Would you consider a six-day school week if you could have a longer summer? Explain why you do or do not like this idea.

❧110❧

How would you feel about shortening the school week to four days a week and adding one more year of school to junior high?

❧111❧

Describe the best teacher you've ever had in school. Was there anything special about this person that made him or her such a good teacher?

❧112❧

Do you think the best teacher you've ever had is the same as your favorite teacher? Explain your answer.

❧113❧

If you were a teacher, what subject would you most like to teach? What grade level would you most like to work with?

❧114❧

Did being in school ever help you discover a talent or ability you didn't know you had?

115

If you had to design a school uniform for students to wear every day, and it could be any type of clothing you want, what would your uniform look like?

116

Would your uniform be the same for both boys and girls? If not, how would it be different?

117

Do you think you should have more time for recess? Would you agree to stay longer in school each day in order to have this time?

118

Have you ever been afraid to speak out in class? If so, explain why you felt this way.

119

If you were asked to design a menu for the cafeteria for one week, what would it consist of? (Be sure to include different foods for each day of the week.)

120

What's the most miserable day you ever had in school? What made it so miserable?

122

Do you know anyone who ever had a more miserable day than you? Describe this person's day.

123

Have you ever done something to help make a teacher's day better? What did you do?

124

What's the nicest thing another classmate has ever done for you?

125

What's the first classroom rule you would make if you were in charge of your present class? What's the second rule you would make?

126

Do you think it would be difficult to enforce these rules with your current class? Why or why not?

127

If you were a teacher and someone in your class was stealing from other students' desks, what would you do to solve the problem?

128

If someone in your class was purposely humming to disturb class, how would you find out who it was if you were the teacher? Once you discovered who the hummer was, how would you stop him or her from disturbing class?

129

Can you think of any holiday you'd like your school to recognize that it doesn't recognize already? Besides having a day off from school, suggest some ways your school might honor this day.

⌒130⌒
What is your favorite subject in school? Why is it your favorite (because you are good at it, the new ideas it gives you, etc.)?

⌒131⌒
If you could eliminate one subject or one activity from your school day, what would it be? Why?

⌒132⌒
If you could add one subject or activity to your school day, what would it be?

⌒133⌒
If you could teach your class for one day, would you change anything? What, if anything, would you change?

⌒134⌒
Do you think you would make a good principal? Why or why not?

⌒135⌒
If you were the principal of your school, what's the first thing you would do for your class?

⌒136⌒
If you were principal, what's the first change you would make in your school?

⌒137⌒
Do you think a school custodian's job is easy? Why or why not?

⌒138⌒
Name one thing you might do to make your school custodian's job easier.

⌒139⌒
If you were a teacher, would you be strict? Why or why not?

⌒140⌒
What's the most interesting project you've ever worked on in science? What did you like most about it?

⌒141⌒
Describe the most interesting story or poem you ever wrote in school. Where did you get the idea for it?

⌒142⌒
Did you ever have a wonderful moment during a school sports event? Describe it.

⌒143⌒
Do you think teaching is a difficult profession? Why or why not?

⌒144⌒
Can you remember the happiest day you ever had in school? Describe it.

When You Wish

⌒145⌒
Are wishes always good? Have you ever wished for something that wasn't good for you? What was it?

⌒146⌒
Did you ever wish for something and regret it later? What was it?

⌒147⌒
Did you ever wish for something good to happen to someone, and it really did? If so, what happened?

⌒148⌒
If you were magically granted three wishes to make your mother's life better, what would you wish for her?

⌒149⌒
If you were magically granted three wishes to make your father's life better, what would you wish for him?

⌒150⌒
If you were granted ten wishes, what would you wish for? (You can't wish for more wishes.)

⌒151⌒
If you could wish for one thing for the President of the United States to help him with his job, what would you wish for him?

⌒152⌒
Have you ever wished about the weather? Why?

⌒153⌒
If you could wish for any weather you like for an entire week, describe it and its effect on your surroundings (include people).

⌒154⌒
If you could wish yourself to be transported anywhere in the world right now, where would you go?

⌒155⌒
If you could wish for anyone in the world to take you to dinner and a movie, who would it be?

☙156☙

If you could have three school wishes, what would they be?

☙157☙

If a little brother or sister (or a small child) asked you how to make a wish come true, what would you tell him or her?

☙158☙

What's the longest you have ever wished the same wish? What were you wishing for? How many times do you think you wished this wish?

☙159☙

Have you ever been disappointed when a wish didn't come true?

☙160☙

Do you believe that making a wish before blowing out the candles on a birthday cake works? Does it matter if it doesn't work?

☙161☙

Have you ever wished for something to save you in an emergency?

☙162☙

Have you ever wished for something specific to happen during a sports event, and it did (for example, a homerun, or a perfect skating routine, or a touchdown, etc.)?

☙163☙

Have you ever wished you were someone else? Whom did you wish to be?

☙164☙

Have you ever wished for a talent or special ability you don't have? Have you ever wished this for someone else?

☙165☙

If you were granted wishes for any two of the following and were certain your wishes would come true, which two would you choose? Love, Health, Success, or Wealth. Explain why you didn't choose the other two.

Desert Island

⌐166⌐

Imagine you must live on a desert island for a year and must rely on yourself and your ingenuity to survive. Try to imagine you are really there, then think carefully about the following questions and try to answer them as honestly as you can.

⌐167⌐

If you could take one person with you to this island, who would it be? (Remember, you must spend an entire year with this person.)

⌐168⌐

If you could take only two books to this island to read for an entire year, what would they be? Why did you choose these books?

⌐169⌐

If you could take only one tool, what would it be?

⌐170⌐

If you could take only two kinds of food, what two specific foods would you take?

⌐171⌐

If you could take one character from a book with you, who would you take?

⌐172⌐

If you could take one character from a television show, who would you take? State the reasons for your choice.

⌐173⌐

If you could take one kitchen appliance with you, what would it be?

⌐174⌐

If you could take ten items of clothing, what would they be? Explain your reasons for these choices.

⌐175⌐

If you had to choose between soap and a toothbrush to take to your island, which would you choose?

◈176◈

If you could take one professional person with you (a doctor, lawyer, architect, scientist, teacher, etc.), who would you choose? Explain the thinking that led to this choice.

◈177◈

If you could have one animal to accompany you to your island, what animal would you take with you?

◈178◈

If you had a cassette player that plugged into a palm tree and worked, what tape would you bring with you if you could only choose one?

◈179◈

If you were with the same person for an entire year, what do you think your biggest disagreement would be on the island?

◈180◈

If you could take one favorite (but useless) possession with you, what would you take (a stuffed animal, a baseball glove, a favorite rock, etc.)? Explain the reason for your choice.

◈181◈

If you could take one musical instrument with you (even if you don't know how to play it yet), what instrument would you take?

◈182◈

If you could take only one game or toy with you, what would you choose and why?

◈183◈

If you could take only one photo with you, which one would you choose and why?

What Would You Do? What Would You Say?

⁓184⁓

Pretend you can be transported back in time to meet any famous person in the world. Who would you choose to meet? What's the first thing you would say to him or her?

⁓185⁓

If this famous person asked you to plan a day for the two of you in your hometown, what would you plan to do? (Describe your imagined day together, including where and what you'll eat, activities, etc.)

⁓186⁓

If you could be transported back in time to meet an American child from long ago, what time period would you choose (for example, Colonial times, the Revolutionary War, the era of Westward Expansion, etc.)? What questions would you ask?

⁓187⁓

If you could ask two of the following famous people one question, what would it be (about their lives, accomplishments, regrets)?

Martin Luther King, Jr.
John F. Kennedy ·
Thomas Jefferson
Susan B. Anthony
Babe Ruth
Tecumseh
Rosa Parks
George Custer
Laura Ingalls Wilder

⁓188⁓

If you could make a list of three or more famous people who are no longer alive and with whom you'd like to have a conversation, who would you put on your list? (Make it as long as you wish.)

⁓189⁓

If you could choose two people from your list and ask them each a question, what would you ask?

⌘ 190 ⌘

If you could actually go into any book or story in the world, which book or story would you choose? What would you do once you were in the story? Would you change any part of it?

⌘ 191 ⌘

If you could be a character in any book in the world, what character would you choose to be? Would you change anything about this character if you could?

⌘ 192 ⌘

If you were handed the script to any movie already made and told you could change the ending to make it the way you'd like it to be, what movie would you choose? How would you change the ending?

⌘ 193 ⌘

If you could telephone the President of the United States directly, and he would answer, what would you say to him? Is there any question you would like to ask him?

⌘ 194 ⌘

If you were elected President of the United States, what are the first three things you would do?

⌘ 195 ⌘

If you could have any pet in the world, what would it be? Why did you choose this animal?

⌘ 196 ⌘

Name a kind act someone has done for you in the past. If this person were standing in front of you right now, what would you say to him or her?

⌘ 197 ⌘

If you were given the opportunity to do a kind act any place in the world right now, where would you go and what would you do?

⌘ 198 ⌘

If you were asked to name three things that are important to you that money cannot buy, what three things would you name? Do you think anyone has ever tried to buy any of these things anyway?

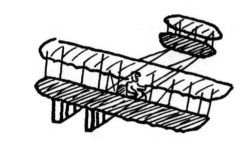

⌘ 199 ⌘

If you could open a door and walk into any historical event, which one would you choose? What is the first thing you would do?

⮞200⮜

If you had to wear one outfit for an entire year (but not worry about being too hot or too cold), what would it be? Describe your outfit from head to toe.

⮞201⮜

If you could invent a robot to do the same three tasks each day for you so that you could have more time to do other things you enjoy, what would these tasks be?

⮞202⮜

What tasks would you program your robot to do for your father?

⮞203⮜

If you could program your robot to do three tasks to help your mother, what tasks would you program it to do for her?

⮞204⮜

Name the first three things you would do if you won $1 million?

⮞205⮜

If you won a lot of money, do you think you would share it with anyone? Who would you share it with?

⮞206⮜

If you were asked to describe the best gift you ever received, what would you say?

Feelings

☙207❧
"*Scared* to death" is a phrase we've all heard at one time or another. Were you ever so frightened you didn't think you'd survive? Tell about your experience.

☙208❧
What's the funniest experience you've ever had?

☙209❧
Describe the happiest moment of your life.

☙210❧
Did you ever have a dream that was so filled with a feeling (anger, sadness, relief) that you felt sure it was really happening? Describe this dream and how it made you feel.

☙211❧
Who is the fairest person you know? How do you feel when you are around this person? Explain how this person acts to make you feel this way.

☙212❧
Is there anything you can't do that you wish you could (spell better, swim, climb a certain tree)? How does it make you feel when you can't do this thing?

☙213❧
Is there anything you can do that others can't (do a split, whistle a whole song, speak Russian)? How does it make you feel to be able to do this thing?

☙214❧
Has anyone ever been jealous of you? What was the person jealous about? How did it make you feel?

☙215❧
Have you ever been so jealous of someone else that you couldn't get it out of your mind? If you could advise someone else about how to get over feeling this way, what would you tell him or her?

☙216❧
Comment on the following statement by Mother Teresa: "The biggest disease today is not leprosy or tuberculosis, but rather the feeling of being unwanted." Do you agree or disagree?

☙217❧
We get angry at ourselves for lots of reasons. When was the last time you were angry with yourself? What was the reason?

☙218☙

When you are angry with yourself, what do you do (for example, stay away from people, explode and shout, play basketball for an hour, etc.)?

☙219☙

Do you act differently when you are mad at yourself than when you are mad at someone else? If so, what do you do that is different when you are mad at someone else?

☙220☙

American critic George Jean Nathan once said: "No one thinks clearly when his fists are clenched." What do you think he meant? Can you think of a time when anger made your thinking unclear?

☙221☙

If a musical instrument could play a feeling, what instrument would play anger? Which one would play hate? Which one would play love? Which one would play peace?

☙222☙

If a color could be a feeling, what color would happiness be? What color would confusion be?
Fill in the blanks:

My _____ is _____
        (feeling)   (color)
like a _____.
               (thing)

☙223☙

If you could offer three suggestions to someone about how to live a happy life, what three things would you suggest?

☙224☙

If you could get a person who was sad to do one activity to get over feeling that way, what would you suggest?

☙225☙

Can you think of a hilarious experience that happened to someone you know?

Early Experiences

☞226☜

Do you recall the feeling you had when you first rode a two-wheeler without training wheels? Does this experience compare to any other experiences you've had lately?

☞227☜

Do you remember what it was like before you learned to tie your shoes? Did anyone ever tie your shoelaces into double knots?

☞228☜

Do you remember your first friend? Who was it? What are some of the things you did together?

☞229☜

Do you remember the first movie you ever saw in a theater? Did you eat popcorn or candy when you were there?

☞230☜

Were you ever frightened by a movie character or creature when you were little? Describe it and what you did.

☞231☜

Did you ever have a dream that happened more than once? Can you describe the most powerful part of the dream?

☞232☜

Do you remember anything about your first day of school? Were you scared? What do you remember most about it?

☞233☜

What was the first thing you wanted to be when you grew up? Have you changed your mind many times since then?

☞234☜

Do you remember the first time you felt proud of yourself? Tell why.

☞235☜

Did you ever do anything heroic when you were little (like call the police during an emergency or save someone by your actions)? If so, describe what happened. If not, did anyone you know perform an important deed at a young age?

⁓236⁓
Did you ever buy something you saw in an advertisement and feel cheated later? What was it?

⁓237⁓
Did you ever get a toy that broke the first time you played with it? Describe what happened.

⁓238⁓
Do you remember the first time you really hurt yourself?

⁓239⁓
Name two of your favorite foods when your were little? Did you have a favorite dessert? Are any of these foods still your favorite?

⁓240⁓
Did you make any odd food concoctions when you were small?

⁓241⁓
When you were small, did you ever eat anything that wasn't food, like a bug or a penny?

⁓242⁓
What's the first holiday you remember?

⁓243⁓
Did you ever do anything when you were little that you wouldn't think of doing now?

⁓244⁓
What was your favorite place to play when you were small? What did you do there? (This place could be inside or outside.)

⁓245⁓
Did you ever make a play area or toy out of something you found around the house, like a cardboard box or a paper-towel roller? What game did you play with your home-made toy or in your homemade place?

⁓246⁓
What was the first game you ever played outside? What was the first game you ever played inside?

⁓247⁓
Do you think you've changed much since you were little? Do you look very different? Do you act differently?

⁓248⁓
Do you ever wish you were younger than you are now? What younger age would you like to be? Explain why.

~249~

Did you ever have a regular chore to do when you were small? Do you remember what it was? Do you have any chores now?

~250~

When is the first time you ever had any money? Where did you get it? What did you do with it? (Remember, it might only be a penny or a nickel!)

~251~

Do you think remembering how you felt when you were a small child will help you to be a more understanding parent if you decide to be a parent someday?

~252~

Does anyone in your family ever tell stories about things you did when you were younger that you can't remember now? Tell one of those stories now.

~253~

How would you describe yourself as a small child—funny, silly, noisy? Have you changed much since then?

~254~

Would you want to have a child like you when you are a parent? Why or why not?

~255~

If you could change anything about yourself when you were small, what would it be? Why would you change this?

~256~

Do you remember when you first learned to read? How did it make you feel?

~257~

What is your earliest memory? Describe it. Why do you think you remember it?

~258~

Can you remember a time long ago when you felt jealousy toward a brother, a sister, or a friend? Describe that event.

~259~

Imagine you are a six-month-old baby in a grocery store. Describe three things from his or her point of view. For example, would people look like giants? Would a common noise seem scary or strange to you?

~260~

Imagine you are a six-month-old baby at the beach. Describe three things from his or her point of view. What would the sand seem like? Would the ocean be frightening?

Real-World Responsibilities

⁓261⁓
Do you currently do any kind of work for money? (It may be at home or somewhere else.) Describe it.

⁓262⁓
If you work, what do you like or dislike most about your job?

⁓263⁓
In your experience, are grown-ups usually happy or unhappy about their jobs?

⁓264⁓
Name one person you know who is happy with his or her job. Why do you think this person likes this job?

⁓265⁓
Do you think a woman or man who stays at home works as hard as one who works outside the home? State your reasons for your answer.

⁓266⁓
Does money have anything to do with how good a person is?

⁓267⁓
If the head of the Department of Labor asked you what you'd consider a good job, what would you say? (Be sure to include the job's duties, hours, and salary.)

⁓268⁓
If the Labor Department asked you if you think Americans work too hard, what would you say?

⁓269⁓
Do you think the work week should be changed to a four-day week with a three-day weekend? Include the reasons for your choice.

⁓270⁓
Name two jobs that you think have a high stress level. Would you consider working at either of these jobs?

⁓271⁓
Booker T. Washington said: "No race can prosper til it learns that there is as much dignity in tilling a field as in writing a poem." Do you agree or disagree?

∼272∼

James M. Barrie, the author of *Peter Pan*, said: "Nothing is really work unless you would rather be doing something else." Do you think a job is always the same as work? Explain your answer.

∼273∼

Do you think going to school and doing homework is your job right now? Explain your answer.

∼274∼

Do you think there are some jobs women shouldn't be allowed to do? Explain you answer. Do you think there are some jobs men shouldn't be allowed to do? Explain your answer.

∼275∼

Do you think everyone has an equal opportunity when applying for a job in America? Explain why you do or do not think so.

∼276∼

How important is having a career that pays a lot of money? Would you consider a career choice based solely on the amount of money you might earn?

∼277∼

Can you think of any worthwhile jobs that don't pay a lot of money?

∼278∼

Do you think it's a good idea for a person your age to work after school or on weekends? Give the reasons for your answer.

∼279∼

What do you think about a weekly allowance? Is it really necessary? Should you have to do chores to earn it? Why?

∼280∼

Some people look down on those who have less money than they do. Do you think this is fair? How would you feel if someone did this to you?

∼281∼

How much money makes a person wealthy?

∼282∼

Do you own an object of great value, even though it isn't worth a lot of money? Describe it.

∼283∼

Do you own anything that you would never sell for any price? Explain why you would never sell this thing.

∼284∼

If you could have any job in the world, what would it be? Would you want to do this forever?

⌒285⌒

In the poem "The War God's Horse Song" by a Native-American Navajo, the author praises the beauty and wonder of his horse in numerous ways: "My horse has a tail like a trailing black cloud...his mane is made of rainbows..." Towards the end of the poem the author states: "I am wealthy from my horse." What do you think he means by wealthy? Are there other ways to feel wealthy besides with money?

⌒286⌒

Can a person be happy without a lot of money? Do you think you could be?

⌒287⌒

Give an example of a family (someone you know or a family from a book) who is happy without a lot of money. What do you think makes them so happy?

⌒288⌒

Can you think of five things you can do to become a better student? What are they?

⌒289⌒

Can you think of five things you can do to become a better brother or sister—or daughter or son? What are they?

⌒290⌒

Do you think it is every American's responsibility to vote? Explain your answer.

⌒291⌒

Pets are a big responsibility. Do you think you are old enough to care for a cat or dog without the help of a grownup? Explain your answer.

⌒292⌒

Can you think of any worthwhile jobs that don't pay *any* money?

Real-World Conflicts

☞293☜

After he takes your lunch money every day, a bigger kid warns that he'll hurt you if you tell anyone. Since you don't believe in fighting to solve problems, what other actions might you take?

☞294☜

Poet Imamu Amiri Baraka said: "Make some muscle in your head but use the muscle in your heart." Do you think his advice might help someone solve a conflict?

☞295☜

After having an argument with someone in your family, who usually makes up first, you or the other person? Explain how making up usually occurs in your family.

☞296☜

What do you think is the best way to handle the following situation: It's your big brother's birthday. Your little brother always gets jealous because he wants presents too. What can you say to your little brother to help him understand?

☞297☜

You are baby-sitting for a smaller child, and she wants to watch a horror movie on television that you don't think is good for her. She swears her mother allows her to watch these movies all the time, but you're not sure and you still feel this movie is too scary for a small child. How would you handle this conflict?

☞298☜

Imagine you are choosing sides for a game of tag and your two best friends are the last ones left. How would you decide which one to choose?

☞299☜

War is the ultimate conflict, but we all face many small conflicts every day when people get on our nerves. We can fight every time we're annoyed or we can find other ways to solve our daily conflicts. Can you name one recent conflict you've had where you chose not to argue or fight? What did you do instead?

☞300☜

Israeli Prime Minister Menachem Begin once asked: "If both sides don't want war, how can war break out?" What are your thoughts on this question? Do you think Prime Minister Begin's question might be applied as well towards the resolution of a fist fight?

⌒301⌒

Do you think a person is weak if he or she chooses to walk away from a disagreement with someone?

⌒302⌒

Have you ever chosen to walk away rather than fight with someone? What are two reasons you can think of for walking away?

⌒303⌒

If you agree to keep a secret and then realize later that it's wrong to keep it, do you think it's okay to change your mind? For example, a friend might ask you to keep a secret about his or her plans to do something dangerous. Is it okay to tell the secret to save that person's life?

⌒304⌒

If a genie offered you a choice between all the money you could ever spend in one lifetime or true love all your life, which would you choose? Tell your reasons for your choice.

⌒305⌒

If you saw someone deliberately teasing or harming a helpless animal, would you tell on him or her? What else could you do?

⌒306⌒

One of your friends was sick the night before an important exam in school and didn't get a chance to study. He or she asks you for an answer during the exam. Would you give it to him or her even if it put you in a terrible position? What else could you do to solve this problem and still keep your integrity?

⌒307⌒

A friend's parent has been offered a better job in another state. Even though the salary is much higher, no one in the family wants to move. If you were the parent, name three things you could do to handle this conflict.

⌒308⌒

A lot of your friends have started smoking cigarettes. You don't want to smoke, but they pressure you more and more to be like them. What can you say or do to solve this problem?

Quotations to Think About

⌒309⌒

Black opera singer Leontyne Price once said: "If you're not feeling good about yourself, what you're wearing outside doesn't mean a thing." What do you think she meant? Can you offer an example from your own experience that proves the truth of this statement?

⌒310⌒

"We never know the worth of water til the well is dry," states an 18th-century English proverb. Can you apply this proverb to anything besides wells and water (friendship, the environment, etc.)?

⌒311⌒

E. W. Howe, an American journalist, provoked thinking when he said: "A thief believes everybody steals." Do you agree? Do you think it's also true that a liar thinks everybody lies? Explain your answer.

⌒312⌒

Calvin Coolidge, the 30th President of the United States, said: "It takes a great man to be a good listener." Do you agree? Do you think it's difficult for some people to be good listeners? When is it most important for you to be listened to?

⌒313⌒

American publisher and essayist Elbert Hubbard said: "Your neighbor is the man who needs you." If you could change the word *man* to *person*, how might this quotation apply to people today?

⌒314⌒

Igor Stravinsky, a Russian composer, once said: "I haven't understood a bar of music in my life, but I *have* felt it." What do you think he meant? Why is the meaning of the words *understood* and *feel* so important to Stravinsky's point of view?

⌒315⌒

"Work is what you do so that some time you won't have to do it anymore," says Alfred Polgar. "Without work all life goes rotten," said French writer Albert Camus. Make up your own definition for work.

⌒316⌒

A Central African proverb states: "War ends nothing." Do you think this is true? If war ends nothing, what *is* ended by war? Do you think war helps stop the bad feelings that cause it?

⌒317⌒

Another proverb from Mongo says: "He who is proud of his clothing is not rich." What do you think this proverb is saying about what it means to be rich?

⌒318⌒

Do you think the philosopher Platonicus, from the first century B.C. meant the same thing when he said: "If I keep my good character, I shall be rich enough"?

⌒319⌒

When Amelia Earhart, American aviator, wrote about her experience as the first woman to make solo trans-Atlantic and Pacific flights, she said: "In soloing—as in other activities—it is far easier to start something than it is to finish it." Do you agree with this statement? From your own experience, can you describe a project that was much easier for you to start than to finish?

⌒320⌒

Madame Chiang Kai-shek, Chinese educator and reformer, once said: "I am convinced that we must train not only the head, but the heart and hand, as well." Nelson Mandela, anti-apartheid activist from South Africa, once said: "A good head and a good heart are always a formidable combination." What do you think Nelson Mandela and Madame Chiang Kai-shek meant by "head and heart?" Do you agree with them?

⌒321⌒

As a young Jewish girl hiding from the Nazis, Anne Frank confided in her diary: "Oh so many things bubble up inside me as I lie in bed, having to put up with people I'm fed up with, who always misinterpret my intentions. That's why in the end I always come back to my diary. That is where I start and finish because Kitty [her diary] is always patient. I'll promise her that I shall persevere in spite of everything, and find my own way through it all, and swallow my tears." Have you ever kept a diary? Do you feel, like Anne Frank, that it was (or is) your most understanding friend at times?

⌒322⌒

In 1977, Bill Cosby, comedian and doctor of education, said: "My grandfather encouraged me by saying, 'Why don't you do what only you can do? Tell about things that happened to you when you were a child.'" Is there something you do well that only you can do? (It could be as simple as calming your little brother or sister with a song.)

☞323☜
What is your opinion of the following quote by former Prime Minister of Israel Golda Meir: "I can honestly say that I was never affected by the question of the success of an undertaking. If I felt it was the right thing to do, I was for it regardless of the possible outcome." Can you think of any other leaders who might have shared Prime Minister Meir's courageous belief?

☞324☜
In one of his poems, Spanish writer Frederico Garcia Lorca wrote: "Green how I love you green Green wind. Green branches..." Can you think of a color you love this much? If you could change more things to your favorite color, which things would you change?

☞325☜
Singer and actress Pearl Bailey once said: "Everybody wants to do something to help, but nobody wants to be first." Can you think of a situation you have experienced where her words are true?

☞326☜
Sojourner Truth—American slave, abolitionist, and reformer—said of herself in 1879: "I'm a self-made woman." Can you think of any other women in history who might have said this about themselves?

☞327☜
Mohatma Gandhi, the great civil rights activist from India, said in 1935: "Nonviolence is the greatest force at the disposal of mankind. It is mightier than the mightiest weapon of destruction devised by the ingenuity of man." What do you think Gandhi meant by this statement? Can you offer one example of how nonviolence can be used as a weapon against violence?

☞328☜
Aretha Franklin, a famous soul singer, once said: "I'm too young to be a legend. I'm still a lady next door. That keeps my feet on the ground." Do you know anybody

famous who seems just like the person next door? If you were famous, do you think you would act differently towards others than you do now?

⇜329⇝

Chief Joseph, a Percé Indian chief, said: "Treat all men alike. Give them all the same laws. Give them all an even chance to live and grow." Do you agree? Tell why.

⇜330⇝

Civil rights leader Martin Luther King, Jr., said: "War is a poor chisel to carve out tomorrows." How is Dr. King using a statement about war to say something important about peace?

⇜331⇝

Do you agree with President Franklin D. Roosevelt's statement: "The nation that destroys its soil destroys itself." Give some examples of how you agree. He also said, "You have nothing to fear but fear itself." Do you agree or disagree?

⇜332⇝

What do you think poet Ralph Waldo Emerson was referring to when he said: "We boil at different degrees?"

⇜333⇝

Do you think St. Augustine was right when he said: "The purpose of all war is peace"? What other purposes can war have?

⇜334⇝

Poet Ralph Waldo Emerson once said: "A hero is no braver than an ordinary man, but he is braver five minutes longer." Humorist Will Rogers offered a very different definition of a hero when he said: "We can't all be heroes because someone has to sit on the curb and clap as they go by." Think about what Emerson and Rogers are saying about heroes, then make up an interesting definition (or two) of your own.

⇜335⇝

Give your interpretation of the following quotation by Martin Luther King, Jr.: "We are not makers of history. We are made by history."

Fun and Fantasy

⌒336⌒

If someone from another planet landed on Earth in the middle of a holiday celebration (such as Halloween, Christmas, Hanukkah, Chinese New Year), what parts of the celebration might appear funny or strange (for example, dragging a tree into the middle of the living room at Christmas time)?

⌒337⌒

If you were asked to design a hilarious school uniform, what would it look like? Remember to be as outrageous as you wish and be sure to include accessories, such as hats, scarves, and jewelry, as well as wild colors.

⌒338⌒

If you could decorate a room in a house to suit only your special needs, what would the room be like? (For example, would there be two refrigerators, or a desk made of chocolate, or a ceiling fan made of ostrich feathers that waves when you say a magic word? Be as fanciful as you wish.)

⌒339⌒

Have you ever accidentally burped at an inappropriate time? Do you recall any situations where this has happened to someone you know?

⌒340⌒

Who is the funniest kid you know? What makes this person so funny?

⌒341⌒

Do you know an adult who is not famous (not on television or in the movies) who can make you laugh? How does he or she do this?

⌒342⌒

Who is your favorite funny person? Give the reasons for your choice.

⁀343⁀

Have you ever been stuck unexpectedly in a place where you didn't want to be stuck (like an elevator)? If so, describe what happened. How did you feel then? Now that you're okay, does it seem funny?

⁀344⁀

Did you ever make a huge mess with a substance that isn't ordinarily used for this purpose (for example, soap lather or food)? If not, did anyone you know ever make such a mess?

⁀345⁀

Did you ever do something you thought your parents would get angry about, but they ended up laughing instead? If so, explain what happened and why they laughed.

⁀346⁀

What's the funniest thing you or someone in your family has ever said?

⁀347⁀

What's the funniest thing you or someone in your family has ever done?

⁀348⁀

Did you ever manage to make someone laugh who usually never laughs? Explain what happened.

⁀349⁀

Some critically ill people claim to have cured themselves with laughter. If you wanted to make yourself laugh, name ten things you would do (for example, read a *Far Side* book of comics by Gary Larson, or watch a Jim Carrey movie).

⁀350⁀

Did you ever get in trouble for laughing? Describe what happened?

⁀351⁀

If you could fill all the swimming pools in the world with any liquid other than water (for example, root beer, or melted cheese), what would you fill them with? What do you think would happen as a result?

⁀352⁀

If you could change any three people in the world into animals, which three people would you choose to change and what animals would you turn them into?

⁀353⁀

If you could change yourself into any inanimate object any time you wished, what inanimate object would you turn into? Give the reasons for your choice.

Grab Bag

ᐅ354ᐊ

If you suddenly became the leader of a small country that had no Bill of Rights for its people, what would be the first three rights you would give them?

ᐅ355ᐊ

If the mayor of your town asked you to submit a description of what you consider the perfect place to live, including your notion of ideal weather, town rules, kinds of schools, and so on, what would you submit to the mayor?

ᐅ356ᐊ

The purpose of commercials on television or radio, or ads in magazines is to sell products to people. Sometimes a commercial promises far more than a product can honestly deliver, for example some ads for weight-loss drinks give the impression that the drink will make everyone who uses it look like a movie star. Can you think of an ad that makes a product seem better than it is? Were you ever tempted by such an ad, even though you knew better?

ᐅ357ᐊ

Do you have a best friend or favorite person you spend time with? What is it about this person that makes him or her your favorite?

ᐅ358ᐊ

Are you anybody's best friend? If you are, why do you think your friend likes you so much?

ᐅ359ᐊ

Many families have special customs or traditions apart from the usual ones of giving gifts at Christmas or Hanukkah, or trick-or-treating on Halloween. Can you think of a custom or tradition as simple as having pancakes every Saturday, going to the dentist each September, or having the youngest child get the first cookie? Explain why you like or don't like this custom.

ᐅ360ᐊ

What kind of weather would best describe your personality (a hurricane, snow, sunshine, fog)? Choose a kind of weather (or more than one, if necessary) that best expresses your personality. Explain the reasons for your choices.

⌒361⌒

What musical instrument is most like you? Choose an instrument that plays your personality (tuba, bells, piano, drums, etc.). Compare the instrument to yourself (how it looks, color, sound, speed or slowness of its rhythms). Be sure to include where it plays the most (solo, orchestra, jazz ensemble, etc.).

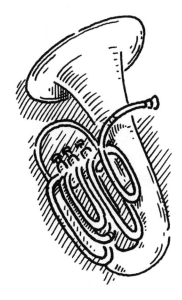

⌒362⌒

If your instrument could play one song that's really you, what would it be?

⌒363⌒

Who is the kindest person you know? Why do you think so? Give an example of this person's kindness.

⌒364⌒

If you were from another planet and the first place your spaceship landed was in a mall, what would your opinion of earthlings be, based upon this first encounter? (Include your impression of the stores, people's behavior, how different people eat and dress, etc.)

⌒365⌒

What is your favorite weather? Why?

⌒366⌒

What is your least favorite weather? Why?

⌒367⌒

What's the best dream you ever had? Describe it.

⌒368⌒

If someone says something nasty to you, what is your usual first response? After you calm down and think about it, do you act differently?

Notes